# Who Will Roar If I Go?

Book I in the *If We're Gone* series

## Paige Jaeger

## Illustrated by Carol Hill Quirk

BQB

Virginia

Published in the United States by BQB Publishing
(an imprint of Boutique of Quality Books Publishing Company, Inc.)
www.bqbpublishing.com

Printed in the United States of America

978-1-945448-15-7 (h)
978-1-945448-16-4 (e)

Library of Congress Control Number: 2018930181

Illustrations by Carol Hill Quirk
Book design by Robin Krauss, www.lindendesign.biz

Editor: Olivia Swenson

We're a cuddly, cute, and an incredible bunch
   Of creatures who enjoy resting just after lunch.
We wrestle and play just like you, every day.
   But some of our friends have been taken away.
Keen eyes, sharp teeth, long claws, and fascinating skin
   Help us survive the trouble we're in.
We need you to care and let us live free.
   Or there will be no more wild animals to see.

3

The King of the Beasts—that's my claim to fame.
   I've got a big crown of hair that's called a mane.
I'm swift and strong and sly, you see,
   And everyone's afraid of me.
Recently I've lost my home;
   There's no savanna on which to roam.
I'm king of this land, don't you know?

   Who will roar if I go?

Lion
Africa

I sure am an enorMOUS creature,
   With ivory tusks my most attractive feature.
For these long, tapered teeth that I hold dear,
   Thousands of friends were lost last year.
No one needs my tusks but me.
   Go make some in a factory.

Elephant
Africa and Asia

The beautiful tiger is my name
And prowling for food is my game.
No one's got a coat like mine—
Black, white, and orange divine.
Everyone loves my stunning, striped hide.
Please leave me alone where I abide.

Tiger
Asia

Like all zebras, my skin is black and white.
 These stunning lines camouflage me day and night.
"Your stripes are amazing," some hunters say,
 And then they take my friends away.
Please leave us here where we multiply,
 And gaze at us next time you wander by.

Zebra
Africa

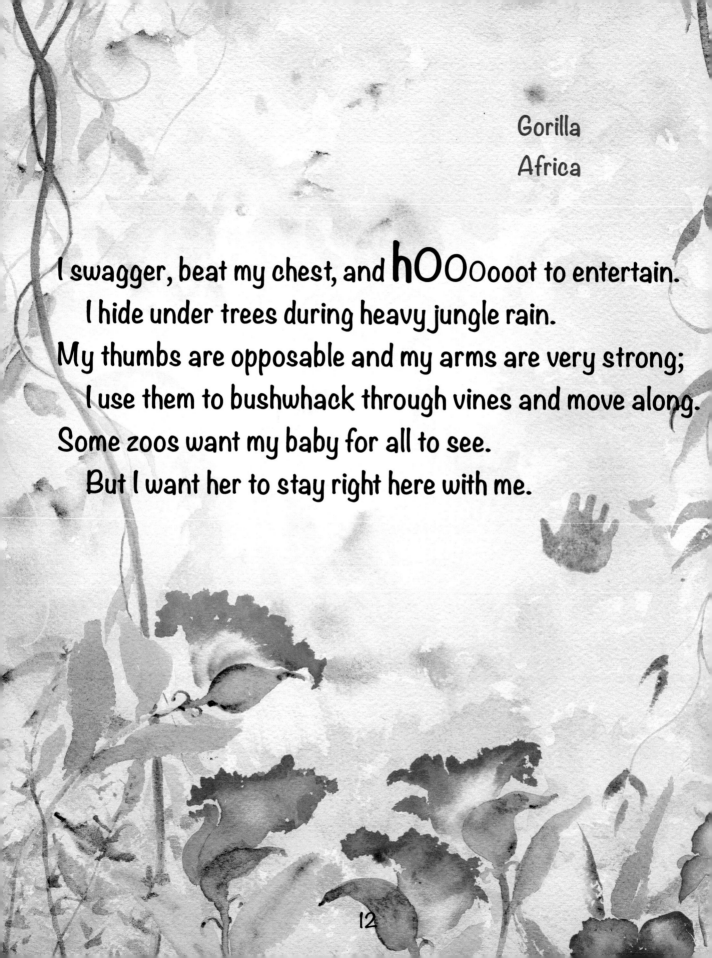

Gorilla
Africa

I swagger, beat my chest, and hOOOoooot to entertain.
   I hide under trees during heavy jungle rain.
My thumbs are opposable and my arms are very strong;
   I use them to bushwhack through vines and move along.
Some zoos want my baby for all to see.
   But I want her to stay right here with me.

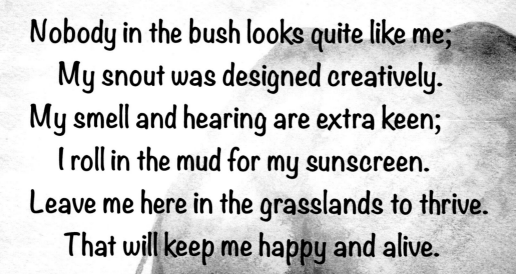

Nobody in the bush looks quite like me;
My snout was designed creatively.
My smell and hearing are extra keen;
I roll in the mud for my sunscreen.
Leave me here in the grasslands to thrive.
That will keep me happy and alive.

Rhinoceros
Africa

Resplendent quetzal really is my name.
 My three-foot tail gives me avian fame.
But I'm vanishing from the forest canopy
 As trees disappear all around me.
Won't you leave our land alone
 So future fledglings have a home?

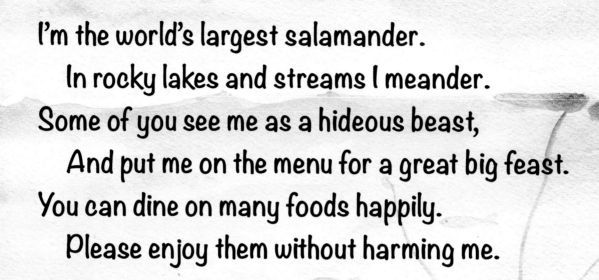

I'm the world's largest salamander.
   In rocky lakes and streams I meander.
Some of you see me as a hideous beast,
   And put me on the menu for a great big feast.
You can dine on many foods happily.
   Please enjoy them without harming me.

Giant Salamandar
China

With brilliant blue wings, my beauty is divine.
I flutter my way through the lush lupine.
Sadly, my terrain is fading fast;
With all the new cities, I may not last.
Please save me a place where I can try
To live in peace as a butterfly.

Blue Karner
North America

No one has a tongue as extendable as mine;
It snares ants and termites in the dirt or on a vine.
Some say that I am ugly and no good,
But that just makes me feel misunderstood.
Tunnels I dig, and trees I climb.
I'd like to stay here for a long, long time.

Pangolin
Australia

22

Panda
China

With black-patchy eyes, I'm chubby and cute.
　I'm a lazy bear who chews bamboo shoots.
Sleeping and munching forests away
　Are the two main activities that fill my day.
But with so little space left for me to graze,
　You'll find me living in the zoo these days.

I'm a Red-crowned Amazon
　　Who wants to fly on and on.
In the trees I love to sing;
　　I sure am a fine-feathered king.
Look at the rainbow crown upon my head!
　　My bright plumage—green, blue, yellow, and red.
Many people think I would make a fine pet.
　　But I belong in the wild, please don't forget.

Red-crowned Amazon
Northeast Mexico

Solitary, swift, and always on the go,
  I wear my spots from head to toe.
With eyes that sparkle and teeth that shine,
  My status is "threatened" because I look so fine.
Some wait in hiding, trying to capture me
  Instead of letting me run wild and free.

Snow Leopard
Asia

Some friends are missing. There are fewer home.
We wander around, feeling sad and alone.
We love where we live and would prefer to stay
Living in our home, not going away.
Before we disappear from this Earth in a blink,
What can you do so that we will not go extinct?

Try to make this world a better place
   by not taking us out of our space.
You can help prevent this travesty,
   So that we'll be wild animals for all to see.
Wildlife is disappearing. What will you do
   If the only place we creatures live . . .
   is in a zoo?
So tell me, are you friend or foe?
   Will you roar before we go?

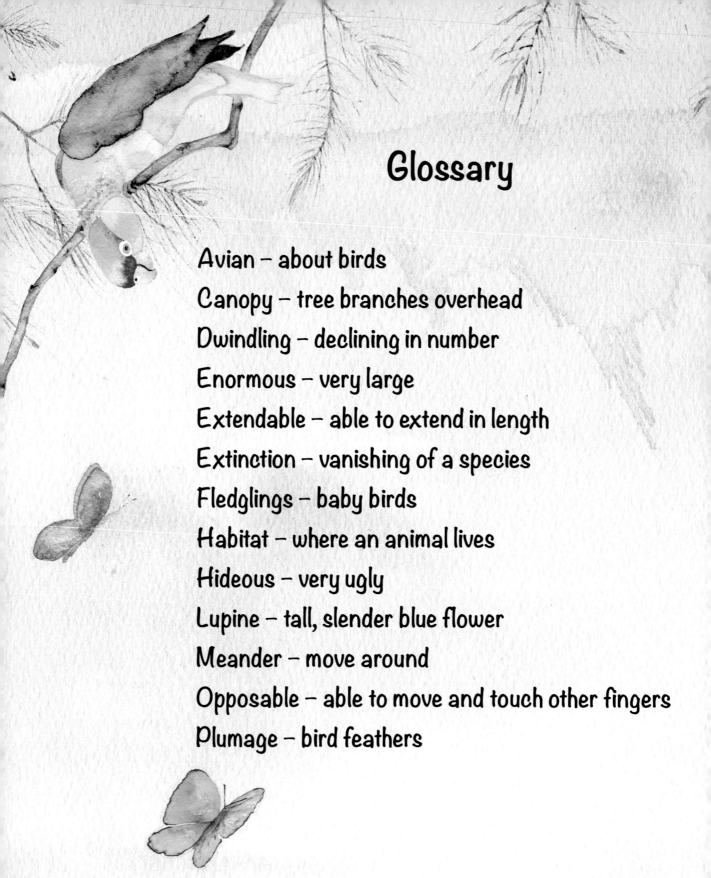

# Glossary

Avian – about birds

Canopy – tree branches overhead

Dwindling – declining in number

Enormous – very large

Extendable – able to extend in length

Extinction – vanishing of a species

Fledglings – baby birds

Habitat – where an animal lives

Hideous – very ugly

Lupine – tall, slender blue flower

Meander – move around

Opposable – able to move and touch other fingers

Plumage – bird feathers

Prowling – to sneakily walk around

Resplendent – shine with splendor

Sly – sneaky

Snout – nose or breathing appendage

Stunning – beautiful

Swagger – to walk slowly with a side-to-side motion

Tapered – long, cone-like shape

Terrain – earth we walk upon

Threatened – at risk, endangered or vulnerable to
   reduced numbers

Thrive – to live very well

Vanishing – disappearing

Vivid – brightly colored

Can you name the animals who leave these footprints?

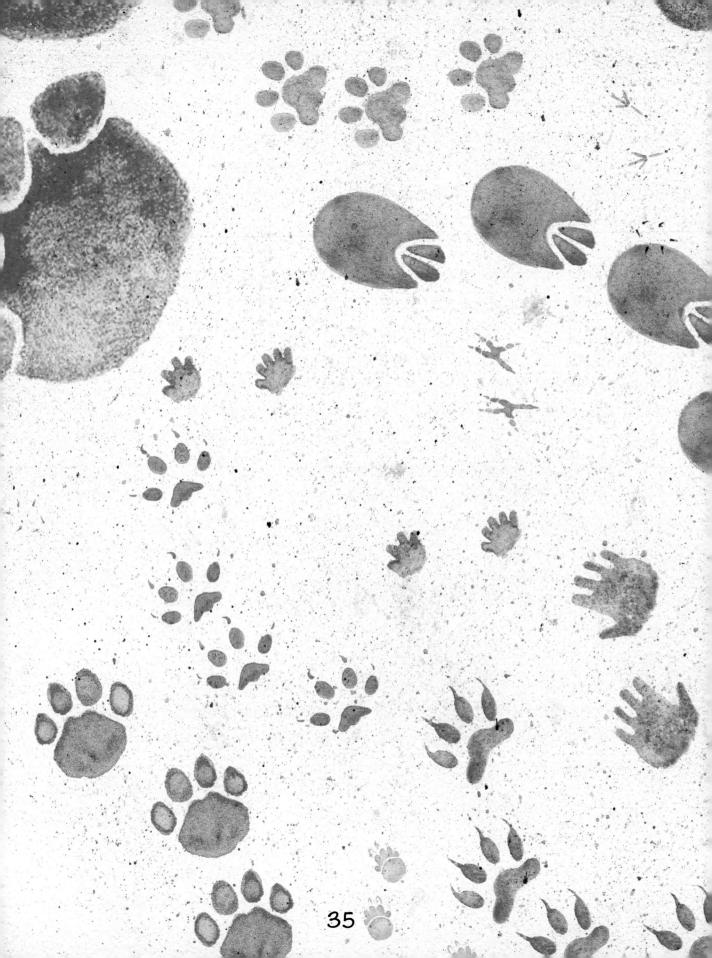

# The Author and Illustrator

## Paige Jaeger - Author

Paige Jaeger is an educator and librarian who has a passion to get students thinking-wondering-investigating and learning.

## Carol Hill Quirk - Illustrator

Growing up surrounded by the natural beauty of New England, its classic architecture and rugged landscapes have inspired Carol to draw. And, with a perennial gardener for a mother and an artistic craftsman for a father, appreciating nature and art was contagious.

Paige and Carol are working on a series of books about the world's endangered species.

Both Paige and Carol support local zoo's endangered species preservation efforts and hope you'll join them in this support by visiting your local zoo often.